FOR BOYS WHO WENT

ADEDAYO ADEYEMI AGARAU

Adedayo Adeyemi Agarau

FOR BOYS WHO WENT

FOR BOYS WHO WENT

Adedayo Adeyemi Agarau

Copyright ©2016 Adedayo Adeyemi Agarau

ISBN: 978-978-547-414-5

All rights reserved.

No part of this book may be reproduced, distributed, stored in a retrieval system or transmitted, in any form or by any means, electronic, electrostatic, magnetic tape, mechanical, photocopying, recording or otherwise without prior written permission from the Publisher.
For information about permission to reproduce selections from this book, write to info@wrr.ng

National Library of Nigeria Cataloguing-in-Publication Data

Printed and Published in Nigeria by:

Words Rhymes & Rhythm Limited
Suite C309, Global Plaza Plot 366, Obafemi Awolowo Way, Jabi District, Abuja, Nigeria.
08169027757, 08060109295
www.wrr.ng

CONTENTS

Comments .... - 6 -
Sea-Girl .... - 10 -
homicide .... - 11 -
rose for your funeral .... - 13 -
a lover's error .... - 15 -
end .... - 16 -
farewell .... - 17 -
SEAMEN .... - 18 -
Dying Again .... - 19 -
Convent Secret .... - 21 -
the thing that drowns us in ourselves .... - 22 -
Not survivors .... - 23 -
For boys who went and never returned .... - 26 -
how to dance .... - 28 -
Timeline .... - 30 -
you may not find me tomorrow .... - 33 -
fresh gods .... - 35 -
LIFEHOUSE .... - 37 -
Body .... - 38 -
Pilgrimage .... - 39 -
ABOUT THE AUTHOR .... - 40 -

DEDICATION

Dedicated to you...

COMMENTS

Agarau's poems not only whisper to the readers' minds, but the verses keep echoing until understanding is attained. He is a poet worth reading.
— ***Kukogho Iruesiri Samson***

Agarau ventures into the murky waters of social criticism with a unique insight into his thematic conceits. He weaves himself into his lines with such finesse that makes him not only empathic with his characters, but he shares their dreams, pains, and, may be, gain. His stylistic propensity is not only fluid but authentic, making his story rich and reaching. His choice of words is unapologetically genuine, making his subject matter real and connecting. Very few writers can seamlessly weave multiple themes with such depth of passion and engagement articulately without certain amount of intrusion as Agarau has done. This collection sets him apart as a poet whose voice will be heard many generations to come.
— ***Funso Oris***

Rich with poignant lines and images that stare back at you in three dimension,

Adedayo has demonstrated what it means to be at the fore of the literary revolution happening in the continent. Every line here dazzles with outstanding brilliance; the dexterity ripples from poem to page; from the first line through the length of the book. The tropes are arresting and liberating, all at once. The themes tuck at the reader's mind with the valid points they raise. Undoubtedly, a fine first offering.

— **Chibuihe-Light Obi**

This right here is a poet of illusion and mirage. In this hour in which anarchy has become the new form of stability, in which sorrow has lost its value, the splendid poems of Adedayo Agarau give us an alternative—a world where normalcy reigns. Where boys learn to throw themselves at the world. Where girls stand their ground. Where parents sing from their palms. Before now, you close your eyes to experience this kind of world, but here you can open those eyes, all thanks to Agarau's gift for the futuristic.
— **D.M. Aderibigbe**

In searching for answers in memories and looking at places and people that are caught up in recent events that has defined our country in recent times. Agarau has written a book of poems, his first offering, that will wake us up into the world as he sees it. From rooms that stink of formaldehyde and death to farewells, he has given us a body of poems that are extraordinary as they are haunting, he has coated reality as he sees it with beauty. This is a wonderful debut from a poet full of promise.

— ***Romeo Oriogun***

*...for boys who went
and never returned*

Sea-Girl

for her

every tide that comes back from surf
brings a memory — of mother,
sister, father, brother, herself mostly
it goes back with the loneliness in her mouth

seashells like sea songs gather
and start a music from her palms
where are you now? what are you doing?
do you miss me?
is home still home?

home is at the mouth of this sea
she sits and watches as a revelation is lost

tomorrow, i may just sink in the belly
of this sea, i may just wake and scrawl
every gill in the fin of marine goddess
or become a goddess

this girl is turning into the image of a moon
in the eyes of night tides
this girl is writing home a broke letter
she fits herself in a bottle
and let tides, like memories, carry her away

homicide

this room stinks of formaldehyde and death;
the pictures of bones, broken like families
of skulls scattered like elephant grasses
at river banks, of spirits gathering to wear
the bodies of new travelers, are rivers
flowing into the eyes.

this room is Benue, a circus of blood thirst
a playground for men who spell their names
by the spread of hectares.
this room is Buni Yadi, Mubi, and elsewhere
an old owl is breaking the song of salt
into indigo, the color of demons holding the body
of school girls with daggers and threats,
this room is not a room anymore
it is Bayelsa, Bakassi Peninsula, Ikorodu,
with gun men eating recurring happiness
of fathered boys, oil moulding itself
into a swell in the body of a country
unsettled like the news
unsettled like ripples
unsettled like itself
this country is a room
filled with bodies
breaking boundaries
for their noses

FOR BOYS WHO WENT

my country is in a green-
walled autopsy room
who killed her?
how? why?

rose for your funeral

A flower grows somewhere in Atlanta
in the middle of the city with a blank sky,
troubled stars lost in the mouth of city priests
on the 14th District.

This flower may have lost home
        Atlanta is no place for roses
something fleshy with sorrow
like my brother's skin
        I was not born with his dress color
        mine came lighter, like fairy or color of the
enemy
at twenty two after my brother's welcome
(at eighteen, after a duel with a rapstar,
                mama's school lover)

she tasted a white man —
      the pound of my father is
      the tooth gap in her mouth

he gave a flower to Jakes for heart break
to his father for leg break
to mother for recovering from coma
after an overdose of depression
a flower for my graduation

at the flower store with friends

FOR BOYS WHO WENT

he plucked a rose from his chest pocket
my father's new girlfriend thought
his hands were taught to pull the trigger
so

everyone in the neighborhood
 has come to his funeral
bearing what grows on their blocks —

roses.

a lover's error

you asked that I suck your
memories away
so i began from the beginning —   navel
i touched it like feathers on the wings of a seabird
you floated and ached in your bones
you shivered and woke in your skin

i nibbled your nipples
and you and your mother
and her mother moaned

she taught you to run
  to disallow little boys from telling you
how your vagina looks

she taught you to wear the cloths
of your father — "men are never available
be scarce my dear, you cannot cut your heart
for a river flowing with dismissal"

i planted my lips on yours
to suck your mother and her mother
and her mother's mother
from your mouth you ached again

at my inability.

FOR BOYS WHO WENT

end

we were boys
learning to throw ourselves to the world
like our kites dangling to wind songs
in the terrain of blue skies

we were tired boys
knitted to our father's names.
how we carved our names
on the sand towers
and gave ourselves big eyes
and big dreams and big faiths
and big distance

when time
became darkness we must
beat with torchlight,
no kite remained,
no sand towers,
no salts,   no soaps,
just us in separate worlds
dancing in the wind.

farewell

    you walked   i stretched
    into my body   into your eyes
                    we both wanted to see
                    what it really meant
                    to be called a bird
                    to course through
                    the skin of a sky or
                    float into the windpipe
                    of a growing god
                    your skin
                    my iris
    is a monument   is a collection
    of fire   of anguish

    i burn   you gnash
        this is not what every book called a lover's body
        they say it is not everything I find here
        what you/i find is not what you/i have come for

    — let's switch places and find peace somewhere else

SEAMEN

ashore:
sea fever

away from home:
longing

home now :
stretching for distances
and spaces that
bring them to the nostrils of water

on sail:
a deep longing for home

at inns on certain nights, in the company of beer and
small-titted lassies:
home and work are at war
and a soldier must find
solace

solitude:
wished
they never left.

Dying Again

memories sip from my veins,
empty me.

I bear the images of how evening fell
 upon the hearts of dwellers,
how we became star hunters waiting for dusk
on dark streets.
I bear the songs of dark rooms, their lyrics
are poetry of war masterminds, how we sang
like the choirs of a red carol,   of blood and
gruesome wars
of men unplugged from their consciences,
how we pleaded for light like weeds living on dews.

empty me here so I can dance
like street whores hitting climax,
I am a mark,   the scars on my face
take me home every night
where we became watchmen waiting on sacred
steps
where we became walls for hands, we became
palms for prayers
where we became monks let to die in dusty
sanctuaries
like winds dying in the throat of a travelling widow,
we became a conglomeration of silences,
a metropolis of bones,

FOR BOYS WHO WENT

a forest of echoes
and echoes
were
what
was left of
home.

I dream of my sister -
the little future we paddled days to see,
the little star in the sky men hunt,
the soft voice in my heart became a
wind rushed through the palms of silence,
how she muffled her poetry through her nostrils,
how she died writing with her feet -
how she dies in my dreams every time I close my
eyes

and I wake again
with my voice
still planted in my anus.

Convent Secret

I was seventeen years old
my life was a mess
— i met the wrong man
i was fecund in darkness
and then the high priest
of our church opened the
doors that led me to the path
of plants. I drank a cup of light
and I ended up in a convent
where women eased my bowels
with their tongues.   I worked
in the orphanage and I took
every girl child into my room
— no girl deserves to learn
about boys or love or heresies
—older women are authors of revival.

the thing that drowns us in ourselves

these things like flood, fire,
tongues, clouds, make us
into caves for our spirits

these people like ghosts shuffled
in a playlist of the bizarre, like stars
arranged in the palms of fortresses
turn us into rivers waiting to overflow a city

these songs like sorrow, pain,
disaster in the face of blue clouds,
sun sinking in the belly of wild children
pulling our veins like harped strings,
are memories crawling up our body
when we remember you father

one morning
you left with promises etched
in the corners of your lips

at dusk we heard the honk
that was not yours anymore
and opened the gate
and your spirit floated to bed.

Not survivors

Our television opened to a documentary
About girls teaching their laps the heat of strange
men in Hong Kong
Two days later, it took us
  through the perils of women sold out
  for marriages in India.

How bad can it be?
How do you measure the joy in your eyes
when the river is unsettling
How do you become a song in the belly of night clouds?

My mother married my father in 1989
He promised to keep her safe
To show her how the fingers of a man
Dives through the planes and hills in the chest of a virgin
He promised to...

I was born in the midst of their midnight melodies
Shut door. Locked eyes. Brawl. My daddy kicked her. She stood to call herself a woman
Then fell into the abyss of the mat
I thought this was love
How mother fell and rose in the morning
As if pain was her nomenclature

FOR BOYS WHO WENT

Is what keeps me.

She taught me silence
How to hold my lips and swallow the songs in my mouth
How to leave the scene and let my shadows stay
How to stay. In pain. In sorrow.

Every morning, I see my mother in the chest of a mirror
Painting yesterday away with her powder
I see how women make excuses for love or lust or war
I see how they gather the dust of fire
And let it burn on fresh ash
I see how my mother breaks
But who else sees...

2007

No other fruit came into my mother's body
And that itself is another war
I mean how would you blame a woman
For every war striking resemblance with genetics?

But dear mother, it's you I have taken after
To hold my tongue and not speak
To break and break and break
Till my bones are memories joining to be a whole story

I hope that when you find me someday
In the middle of my father's thighs
You will realize that we are mates now
We are fighting the same war
We are not survivors
We are not dead cadavers either
We are a mother and her twelve year old child
dying of silences.

For boys who went and never returned

here is a bed for your absence
for lizards to crawl
for silky silence
for the names of the girls
who have stretched for you — do you still
remember?

for songs dissolving in the mouth of your mothers
for songs dissolving in the mouth of your mothers
for songs I have tasted are bitter like absence
for songs I have tasted are bitter like battlefields

for dreams you left behind
are footnotes for mothers to read
when insomnia holds their eyelids
they are lyrics for chants
they are placards for notice
    "who has found our children
      they have these dreams and those
      if anyone else is living them
      please call the police
      it's plagiarism"

for homes are broken for suns
for suns are weary of waking
and dying in the mouth of widows
for widows are by their windows

eyes stretched beyond their skulls
waiting for drums that would lead them
to home calls

for cities uphill are sliding
into the palms of underfed gods
they are looting your mothers

for mothers are broken
like distuned strings for you

for fathers went like this
and never returned too

how to dance

after mesioye

they say the night does not speak
but your tongue has a moon
and it runs ashore like a ship
embittered with fever

you cannot look up to your father
without walking into a room of haunting pictures
where you become a stone, a cannon, a revolution
waging war in distant cities

you have sorrow, i see it in your pocket
you have not visited yourself in a while
you have not opened the windows
in the room where you became fire
and river and lake

but wait, throw yourself in a song
your mother comes into scene
her hands open a verse in passenger's circle
and your demons begin to sip
touch your feet for revival
shut your eyes and see
your father as he smiles

the breast pocket of night clouds open

winds slide into your jeans
tiny ray of moonlight touches your skin
sway. sway.   sway.

lose yourself in this forest of becoming
you must find happiness in every soul
every demon must forget your name
or remember to call you formidable

when you are done losing yourself
throw you hands in the air
left or right,   any will do,
dab like angels blowing the trumpet

Timeline

1999, my country decided to try a new style
1999, safe sex!
1999, my country and the man decided what position fit
1999, we dropped dominance

2000, my country found a name on the atlas
2001, I had my first birthday party
2001, I was 6 when my father bought his Ericsson
a gadget that caused us to fast then prey
at the sight of our neighbors crunching lunch
2001, there were fireflies in the eyes of Benue
the soldiers that were sent to save the land
sank about two hundred beneath their boots
abduction found itself in the dictionary of my country
mothers flung their wrappers,   children sold their eyes
fathers, gone, gone, gone.

2002, a bomb blasted in Lagos
my country found her name again
                              in a cemetery

2003, a monkey climbed the same tree twice
2004, nothing happened but the oil city

became a vein of blood. You cannot go to Port Harcourt
unless you have a gun for a tongue and daggers for teeth
unless you bore on your palms the head of another man
unless oil floated in your artery
2005, 2006, 2007,
a ghost learnt the art of leadership
and sat on the teeth of ghouls
he later floated into a tombstone in 2010

bayelsa has always had good luck
so in 2009, a pastor with a church
beside an oily river gave a testimony

two kings ruled in 2009
one was breathing slowly
beneath a UV lamp
the other was receiving orders
from old boys of the Deltan golf course

2009, Boko Haram entered the body of my country
took two cities and ate them at once

2010, our president died again

2011, Boko Haram, 2012, 2013, 2014
walked into a school and snatched dreams

from the eyes of two children, three girls and four women

We started searching later
because a boy is at the boot camp
pleading for tomorrow

2015, otuweke became home for
old boys in camou suit

2016,
we are back in 1999 or 1983 or 1960
recession, hunger, joblessness
we are somewhere near a brighter future.

Adedayo Adeyemi Agarau

you may not find me tomorrow

this is my heart breaking like the tides in summer
every time i hold you, my skin dissolves into a
goodbye song

abidemi, the night brings a bowl to fetch me from
daylight
i touch my lips, they would not stop learning the
chords of dirge
angels are here and there waiting for harvest,
i am going into homes bleeding of memories
this is me fibbling your name on my tongue

my mother's demons left a trait of her in my blood
sadness corrodes my heart,   anguish stops to prey
my blood fumes of decay,   oxygen weaves into
dead oxides
immunity dies at war, i am shattering
i am shattering, immunity dies at war

abidemi, you may not find me tomorrow
these dreams teach how to float
into caves where women hang their breath
where leukemia punctures radiant smiles
when the sun melts into a raging cannon ball
leaking into my blood. pint. pint. pint. pint.

hold yourself and learn the strength of great walls

FOR BOYS WHO WENT

tomorrow, i may find slight breath again
but i swear, it's just to say goodbye,
the doctor said i'm damned
and i have seen darkness in my dreams,

abidemi, we may never hold words together again

fresh gods

the song in my mouth is
waiting to split like Biafra and
Nigeria, for boys falling into
our prayers like raindrops in
the chest of Ibadan

one song is a dirge
    and gods do not die
but when bullets rip our fleshes and opens a book
where we read the crimsoned-names of other black
boys
who fell by the pull of triggers,
we burn our eyes to bury their names

the other song is of revolution: a chant—
for Sanders, Castillo, Alton,
and #blacklivesmatter
even ashes are burning again
and the eyes of the night is peeling its skin like
    nowhere is safe to be anything black

somehow we plant the bodies of these fresh gods
on newsstands and national papers
and say to young boys:
do not raise your hands
do not drop it, just sink into a prayer
when you sight a white man in funeral dress

FOR BOYS WHO WENT

aiming at you
for shooting practice.

LIFEHOUSE

for Ehizogie

run into your poems
when you need a nose

there, you have a small Fulani boy
with bowl in hand,
a fainting smile,
button of his shirt have fallen like leaves
from trees in harmattan

look into his eyes
and ask him how it is to be alive

what did he say?

Body

for Romeo

How does it feel to walk alone
in vacant spaces
do you hear your voice talk back?
do you hear your dreams creak like
your skin?

my body is home to songs
you may touch my eyes if you do not believe
you may hold my feet for a while
if you must check the places I've been
My body is no home to me
It's for boys broken likes split river
It's for burnt men whose ashes are butterflies
colouring the graves of mad men
It's for another poet finding his voice in a pile of old
books
for Ikare boys and their windows
for widows and their retired laps
for tongues drowning like watered eyes
for other people a poem cannot describe.

I live in a body that's not mine
where do you live?

Pilgrimage

When you get
        to your mother
tell her how long
        it took you
to find home.

ABOUT THE AUTHOR

Adedayo Adeyemi Agarau is a Nigerian food nutritionist from the uphill area of Oke Agbo in Ijebu Igbo, Ogun state. He was born in Ibadan.

Adedayo started writing poetry in 2013. He has won several writing awards including the *'What Can Words Do'* challenge in 2013, the *Pulse Student Poetry Prize* and the *Tony Tokunbo Fernandez International Poetry Prize* in 2014, the *Brigitte Pooirson Poetry Contest* (July) in 2015 and the *Eriata Food Poetry Contest* in 2016.

In 2013, he compiled a collection of political poetry, *Epistle of Lies*, which featured a hundred poets. Adedayo's words have been published on *Kalahari, Sankofa, WRR, African Writers, Praxis Magazine*, and several other platforms.

He lives in and Writes from Ibadan.

In this hour in which anarchy has become the new form of stability, in which sorrow has lost its value, the splendid poems of Adedayo Agarau give us an alternative—a world where normalcy reigns.
— **D.M. Aderibigbe**

...

Agarau's poems only whisper to the readers' minds, but the verses keep echoing until understanding is attained. He is a poet worth reading.
—**Kukogho Iruesiri Samson**

Adedayo Adeyemi Agarau is a Nigerian writer and food nutritionist from the uphill area of Oke Agbo in Ijebu Igbo, Ogun state. He was born in Ibadan.

Adedayo started writing poetry in 2013. He has won several writing awards including the What Can Words Do challenge in 2013, the Pulse Students Poetry Prize and the Tony Tokunbo Fernandez International Poetry Prize in 2014, the Brigitte Poirson Poetry Contest (July) in 2015 and the Eriata Oribhabor Food Poetry Contest in 2016.

In 2013, he compiled a collection of political poetry, Epistle of Lies, which featured a hundred poets. Adedayo's works have been published on Kalahari, Sankofa, WRR, African Writers, Praxis Magazine, and several other platforms.

He lives in and writes from Ibadan.

COVER DESIGN: **KUKOGHO IRUESIRI SAMSON**

www.ingramcontent.com/pod-product-compliance
Lightning Source LLC
Chambersburg PA
CBHW031507040426
42444CB00007B/1235